# VOICES

## Poems About Friendship, Feelings & Growing Up in Middle School

# UNLOCKING VOICES

## Poems About Friendship, Feelings & Growing Up in Middle School

### JAMIE JOY

honking good books for wobbly wings

With profound thanks to the team of illustrators at Giggle Goose Press who helped with the Illustrations and Cover for this book

Loved unlocking your voice with "Unlocking Voices"? Share your thoughts in a review and help others discover this book!

No part of this publication may be reproduced, stored in a retrieval system or transmitted in any form or by any means, electronic, mechanical, photocopying, recording, or otherwise without written permission of Giggle Goose Press.

Copyright © 2024 Giggle Goose Press
All rights reserved
Paperback

# Table of Contents

| | |
|---|---|
| Introduction | 1 |

## the cafeteria chronicles

| | |
|---|---|
| Finding Your Voice (Social Media) | 4 |
| Body Image | 5 |
| First Love (Awkward) | 6 |
| Fitting In (Feeling Different) | 7 |
| Friendship Conflict (Communication) | 8 |
| From Texting to Talking (Communication) | 9 |
| Squad Goals & Standing Out (Finding Your Tribe) | 10 |

## the locker laughs

| | |
|---|---|
| The Lunchroom Shuffle | 12 |
| The Great Homework Hideout | 13 |
| Test Day Jitters (But Not Really) | 14 |
| Weekend Warriors | 15 |

## the backpack blues

| | |
|---|---|
| Don't Sweat the Sweatpants (Dealing with Social Pressures) | 17 |
| Teacher Troubles & Triumphs (Finding Mentors) | 18 |
| Homework Hassle & Finding Balance (Juggling Responsibilities) | 19 |

## the mirror within

| | |
|---|---|
| Mirror, Mirror (Body Image) | 21 |
| The Pressure to Fit In (Finding Your Voice) | 22 |
| The "Shoulds" and "Shouldn'ts" (Finding Your Path) | 23 |
| The Power of "Yet" (Growth Mindset) | 24 |

## the heartbeat hustle

| | |
|---|---|
| First Crush Confusion (Butterflies & Awkwardness) | 26 |
| Friend Zone Blues (Unrequited Feelings) | 27 |
| The "What Ifs" (Overcoming Fear & Doubt) | 28 |
| Author's Notes | 29 |

# Introduction

Hey there, middle school warriors!

Ever feel like you're living in a whirlwind of textbooks, cafeteria chaos, and trying to figure out who you are exactly? (Spoiler alert: it's totally normal!) Don't worry, you're not alone in this wild ride called middle school. My name is Jamie Joy, and I was once a middle schooler myself – braces, awkward crushes, and all the glory that comes with it.

Now, I'm here as your unofficial guide to navigate this amazing, sometimes confusing, and definitely unforgettable time. "Unlocking Voices" is a collection of poems that dives headfirst into the world of growing up, capturing all those unspoken emotions that swirl around in your head.

Think of it as a secret decoder ring for deciphering all the ups and downs of middle school life. Inside these pages, you'll find poems about:

The rollercoaster of friendships: From best friend squabbles to unshakeable bonds, we'll celebrate the power of friendship (and how to navigate those occasional disagreements).

The cafeteria chronicles: Spilled lunches, hilarious mishaps, and the unspoken language of lunchtime. (FYI, the coveted corner table is definitely a power move!)

<u>Triumphs and test-day jitters:</u> We'll celebrate your wins, big and small, and offer a secret weapon to conquer those test-day butterflies.

<u>First crushes (and the awkwardness that comes with them):</u> Butterflies in your stomach, sweaty palms, and wondering if they even notice you exist. (Spoiler alert: they probably do!)

<u>Finding your voice:</u> Middle school can feel like everyone else is shouting, but this book will help you discover your own unique voice and shout it loud and proud!

So grab a cozy corner, settle in, and let's unlock those voices! These poems are like messages in a bottle, sent straight from someone who understands (and remembers!) what it's like to be in your shoes.

This is just the beginning! I've got a whole bunch of stories and poems waiting to be shared, so if you enjoy this one, keep an eye out for more adventures in the future!

Now, enough chit-chat, let's get this party started! Turn the page and get ready to unlock the amazing voice that's already inside you.

Here's to your middle school journey (may it be filled with laughter, learning, and awesome discoveries!),

Jamie Joy

the cafeteria chronicles

"Middle school cafeterias: a place where friendships are forged, lunches are spilled, and memories are made."

# Finding Your Voice

Likes and comments, a constant display,
The pressure to curate, a perfect ballet.
But filters can't capture the depth of a soul,
Disconnect to reconnect, make yourself whole.

# Body Image

Society's standards, a picture they paint,
But your worth shines brighter, beyond any faint.
Love the body you're in, every curve and each line,
It's uniquely yours, a masterpiece, truly divine.

At Jake's Pool Party

# First Love

Butterflies erupt, a nervous display,
When your crush walks by, what do you say?
Stuttering hello, a shy little wave,
Hoping they noticed, not feeling brave.

# Fitting In

Surrounded by faces, all seemingly bold,
The pressure to conform, a story untold.
Embrace your uniqueness, let your colors fly free,
The right people will find you, the ones who truly see.

*Daren's first day at school after Summer*

# Friendship Conflict

Angry words sting, a misunderstanding deep,
Friendship's melody, turned into a sleep.
Take a deep breath, let your feelings be known,
Honest apologies, help friendships to grow.

# From Texting to Talking

Emojis and memes, a digital facade,
Honest conversations, where feelings are laid.
Pick up the phone, vulnerability's key,
Deepen connections, for you and for me.

# Squad Goals & Standing Out

Cliques rule the hallways, a hierarchy set,
But your worth isn't measured, by who you haven't met.
Embrace your quirks, let your colors fly free,
Your true tribe awaits, the ones who truly see.

the locker laughs

*"Between classes and tests,
there's always time for a locker laugh or two."*

# The Lunchroom Shuffle

Trays clatter and crash, a lunchroom symphony,
Spilled milk rivers flowing, a creamy tragedy.
Dodging flying carrots, and mystery meat surprise,
Lunchtime adventures, with laughter in our eyes.

Lunchtime Craziness

# The Great Homework Hideout

Papers scattered, a textbook avalanche,
Desperate search for answers, a mental rampage.
Under the bed, a fort of pillows we weave,
Homework forgotten, dreams we believe.

# Test Day Jitters

Pencils sharpened, erasers prepped and clean,
Test day arrives, a nervous scene.
But wait, a secret weapon, hidden from view,
A lucky charm, in shades of blue.
Confidence soars, with a silent wink,
This test won't stand a chance, I don't think!

# Weekend Warriors

School bell rings, a glorious sound,
Freedom's embrace, on happy ground.
Bikes and skateboards, a blur of delight,
Weekend adventures, shining ever so bright.
Pizza parties, with friends so true,
No homework worries, just me and you.

the backpack blues

*"Juggling homework, friendships, and finding your place: the challenges and triumphs of growing up."*

# Don't Sweat the Sweatpants

Fashion magazines, with models so thin,
Whispering "flaws," a never-ending din.
But confidence blooms, from the inside out,
Don't sweat the sweatpants, let your true self shout.
Be you, be bold, be wonderfully you,
There's nothing more stylish, than staying true.

# Teacher Troubles & Triumphs

Lectures and deadlines, a teacher's firm hand,
Pushing your limits, to help you understand.
Respect and patience, pave the way for growth,
Lessons learned deeply, nurtured and sowed.
But sometimes, a teacher, just doesn't click,
Don't fret, there's another, with a helpful trick.
Keep searching, keep learning, with an open mind,
The perfect mentor, you'll surely find.

# Homework Hassle & Finding Balance

Textbooks and tests, a never-ending race,
Extracurriculars calling, leaving little space.
Sports practice late, and drama club woes,
Homework piles high, where does the time go?
Prioritize passions, make time for you too,
Balance is key, to dreams coming true.
A schedule's your friend, a helpful tool,
To manage your week, and stay cool.

the mirror within

*"Looking in the mirror is more than
just seeing your reflection, it's about discovering
who you truly are."*

# Mirror, Mirror

Reflected image, a critical stare,
Flawlessly flawless, that's not who we are.
Imperfections and all, a beautiful design,
Embrace your uniqueness, truly one of a kind.
Inner beauty shines, brighter than the rest,
Love and accept yourself, you're truly blessed.

# The Pressure to Fit In

Surrounded by faces, all seemingly bold,
The pressure to conform, a story untold.
But your voice matters, unique and so true,
Don't silence your song, let it shine through.
Be you, be brave, break free from the mold,
The world needs your light, a story to be told.

My First Solo Performance

# The "Shoulds" & "Shouldn'ts"

"Should" you be a doctor, a lawyer, a star?
Society's whispers, reaching afar.
Explore your passions, the fire within,
A musician, an artist, a writer to win?
Don't let expectations, chart your life's course,
Find your own purpose, a beautiful force.

# The Power of Yet

Stumbled on the test, a crumpled score,
Feels like hitting rock bottom, wanting more.
Doubt whispers a lie, "You'll never succeed,"
But a tiny voice rises, a powerful seed.

It speaks in a whisper, firm yet kind,
"This isn't the end, just a bump you can find.
The power of 'yet' shines ever so bright,
It means you're still learning, with all your might."

Didn't make the team, a tear escapes your eye,
But the 'yet' voice whispers, "Give it another try.
Practice makes progress, with dedication's flame,
The goal may seem distant, but it's not a game."

Friendship on the rocks, a hurtful word stings,
The 'yet' voice reminds you, forgiveness brings.
Open communication, a bridge to repair,
Friendship's strong foundation, a bond to share.

So next time you stumble, or feel like you fall,
Remember the 'yet,' it answers your call.
It's the power of learning, the strength to persist,
Unlocking your potential, with a determined fist.

the heartbeat hustle

"Navigating friendships, crushes, and growing up
can make your heart skip a beat, but it's
all part of the beautiful journey."

# First Crush Confusion

Butterflies erupt, a nervous display,
When your crush walks by, what do you say?
Stuttering hello, a shy little wave,
Hoping they noticed, not feeling brave.
Thoughts in a tangle, a jumbled up mess,
Wishing for courage, to impress, impress.
Maybe a smile, a friendly hello,
First crush feelings, where will they go?

# Friend Zone Blues

Stuck in the friend zone, a heart feeling blue,
Wishing for more, but what can you do?
Honesty is best, let your feelings be known,
Move forward with grace, even if you're alone.
True friendship's a treasure, a bond to hold tight,
Even if romance fades, a friendship takes flight.

# The "What Ifs"

"What if I fail?" whispers fill the air,
Fear holding you back, from dreams you can share.
Take a deep breath, and silence the doubt,
Believe in yourself, you'll surely figure it out.
Step outside your comfort zone, with courage so bright,
Embrace the unknown, and take flight, take flight.

# Author's Notes

Part 1: The Cafeteria Chronicles

Finding Your Voice (Social Media): This poem explores the pressure to curate a perfect online persona. It's a reminder that true connection comes from authentic interactions, not filtered portrayals.

Body Image: Society often bombards us with unrealistic beauty standards. This poem encourages self-love and appreciation for your unique body.

First Love (Awkward): First crushes can be a whirlwind of emotions and awkward encounters. This poem captures the butterflies, nervousness, and hope that come with those early experiences of love.

Fitting In (Feeling Different): Feeling like you don't belong is a common experience in middle school. This poem encourages you to embrace your individuality and find your true tribe.

Friendship Conflict (Communication): Friendships aren't always smooth sailing. This poem highlights the importance of communication and honest apologies in resolving conflicts.

From Texting to Talking (Communication): While texting is convenient, there's something special about face-to-face communication. This poem encourages deeper connections through open conversations.

Squad Goals & Standing Out (Finding Your Tribe): Finding your true friends, the ones who accept you for who you are, is an important part of growing up. This poem celebrates the power of friendship and individuality.

Part 2: The Locker Laughs

The Lunchroom Shuffle: Middle school cafeterias can be chaotic places! This poem captures the humorous mishaps and messy moments that can happen during lunchtime.

The Great Homework Hideout: Sometimes, escaping the pressure of homework is just what you need. This poem injects humor into the universal struggle of getting schoolwork done.

Test Day Jitters (But Not Really): Test anxiety is real, but this poem takes a lighter approach, reminding us that a little humor and a positive attitude can go a long way.

Weekend Warriors: School can be tough, but weekends are for fun! This poem celebrates the freedom and adventures that come with the weekend.

Part 3: The Backpack Blues

Don't Sweat the Sweatpants (Dealing with Social Pressures): Social pressure to conform is strong in middle school. This poem encourages you to embrace your individuality and wear what makes you feel comfortable.

Teacher Troubles & Triumphs (Finding Mentors): Teachers play a significant role in our lives. This poem acknowledges that not all teacher relationships are perfect, but also highlights the importance of finding mentors who inspire and support you.

Homework Hassle & Finding Balance (Juggling Responsibilities): Juggling schoolwork, extracurricular activities, and social life can be overwhelming. This poem offers tips on finding balance and prioritizing your time.

Part 4: The Mirror Within

Mirror, Mirror (Body Image): Our reflection in the mirror can sometimes be our harshest critic. This poem encourages you to focus on your inner beauty and accept yourself for who you are.

The Pressure to Fit In (Finding Your Voice): It's important to find your voice and express yourself authentically. This poem encourages you to be yourself and not conform to expectations.

The "Shoulds" and "Shouldn't"s (Finding Your Path): Don't let others dictate your future. This poem encourages you to explore your passions and find your own unique path in life.

The Power of Yet (Growth Mindset): Facing setbacks and challenges is a normal part of growing up. Sometimes, these experiences can leave us feeling discouraged or defeated. "The Power of Yet" reminds us that the word "yet" holds immense power. It signifies that something may not be achieved yet, but it doesn't mean it's impossible.

This poem celebrates the power of perseverance and a growth mindset. It encourages you to embrace the learning process, even when things don't go your way. Remember, every setback is an opportunity to learn, grow, and become stronger. The power of "yet" ignites the spark of possibility, reminding you that with dedication and effort, you can achieve your goals and overcome any obstacle.

Part 5: The Heartbeat Hustle

First Crush Confusion (Butterflies & Awkwardness): Navigating first crushes can be confusing and awkward. This poem captures those mixed emotions and encourages you to embrace the experience.

Friend Zone Blues (Unrequited Feelings): Sometimes our feelings aren't reciprocated. This poem acknowledges the pain of rejection but also highlights the importance of valuing friendships.

The "What Ifs" (Overcoming Fear & Doubt): Self-doubt can hold us back from achieving our dreams. This poem encourages you to silence your fears and take a leap of faith.

Made in the USA
Monee, IL
26 July 2024